'Imagine the ideal sh
lived between land, sk

The Times

'Wonderfully stirring . . . The great pleasure of *Land's Edge* is not just the dissection of his own love of the sea but also the flint-sharp evocation: he can fill your nostrils with the salty breeze . . . His is a book to read and reread . . . its reflections are beautiful, urgent and filled with awe.' *Mail on Sunday*

'The beach, the "verandah" at the edge of the continent, is half-fantasy, half-horror story. Winton is brilliant at exploring this ambiguity . . . I gobbled up this short but shimmering book in one windswept afternoon.'

Independent

'A timeless meditation on place and the intimate affirm-ation of a writer's life lived on his own terms.' *Time*

'In this slim, poetic memoir, Winton picks apart his lifelong attraction to the ocean . . . compelling . . . the ocean's twin allure of fear and freedom is what Winton captures so well.' *Sunday Times*

Land's Edge

TIM WINTON has published twenty-five books for adults and children, and his work has been translated into twenty-eight languages. He has won Australia's Miles Franklin Award four times (for *Shallows, Cloudstreet, Dirt Music* and *Breath*) and twice been shortlisted for the Booker Prize (for *The Riders* and *Dirt Music*). He lives in Western Australia.

Tim Winton

Land's Edge

A Coastal Memoir

PICADOR

First published 1993 by Plantagenet Press
First published in paperback 1993 by Pan Macmillan Australia

This edition first published in the United Kingdom 2012 by Picador

First published in paperback 2014 by Picador
an imprint of Pan Macmillan, a division of Macmillan Publishers Limited
Pan Macmillan, 20 New Wharf Road, London N1 9RR
Basingstoke and Oxford
Associated companies throughout the world
www.panmacmillan.com

ISBN 978-1-4472-0309-4

1 3 5 7 9 8 6 4 2

A CIP catalogue record for this book is available from the British Library.

Printed and bound by CPI Group (UK) Ltd, Croydon, CR0 4YY

Visit **www.picador.com** to read more about all our books
and to buy them. You will also find features, author interviews and
news of any author events, and you can sign up for e-newsletters
so that you're always first to hear about our new releases.

We speak of course of that narrow
strip of land over which the ocean waves
and moon-powered tides are masters – that
margin of territory that remains wild despite
the proximity of cities or of land surfaces
modified by industry.

W. J. Dakin – *Australian Seashores*

Life's short – go surfing!

Bumper sticker

Chapter One

On a low tide Monday afternoon just short of my thirty-third birthday the winter sun finally comes out to burn the sky clear of cloud and the kids and I gallop onto the beach to play. An easterly wind spikes out across the broad lagoon flattening the sea and running rashes across it in cold gusts. Under the sun the water shows its mottling of deeps and shallows, black and turquoise, reef and sand, dark and light, its coming and its going. The blunted swell butts against the barrier reef in feeble lines that lie down before the wind. Way out, the horizon looks like a ripsaw. At first glimpse of the Indian Ocean I stop running and feel the relief unwinding in my chest, in my neck and shoulders. Dinghies twist against their moorings. Gulls scatter before the blur of my insane kelpie. Two days off the plane, I am finally home.

The sand is cold beneath our bare feet and the dunes damp and spicy with marram grass and saltbush. We wheel down the wind hollows between the dunes, yelling and fooling about, shaking off the confines of the house, the stalemates and frustrations of winter indoors. The sun slants finely on our necks, barely felt, lighting the hard white beach to squinting point, to the momentary point of summer.

Down at the low-water mark, at the scalloped edges of the shore, the water is gigglingly cold. Clouds rise around our feet. The four of us hold hands and bend like a sail, raucous in the east wind, laughing with shock.

The kids fall to digging and damming and sculpting. They wet the knees of their trousers. They sniff back the gunk of their head colds and go quiet with concentration over moats and walls while I stand there in the water with my feet going numb and my mind drifting in a kind of fugue state that only comes to me here.

There is no one else around. I flinch at the sound of a school of whitebait cracking the surface a few metres away. It's alive out there. After the still, exhausted Aegean, where nothing moves but the plastic bags, it seems like a miracle. Call it jet lag, cabin fever, but I am almost in tears. There is nowhere else I'd rather be, nothing else I would prefer to be doing. I am at the beach looking west with the continent behind me as the sun tracks down to the sea. I have my bearings.

—

Like most Australians I have spent much of my life in the suburbs. I was raised in the Perth suburb of Karrinyup. A quarter acre, a terracotta roof, a facade knocked out by some bored government architect, a Hills Hoist in the back yard and picket fences between us and the neighbours. It was the sixties and the street was full of young families, State Housing applicants, migrants from Holland and Yugoslavia and the English north – foot soldiers of the great sprawl trying to make our way in the raw diagram of streets we slowly filled to make a new neighbourhood. I lived there happily for twelve years but I do not dream of that house.

As an adult – well, a child bridegroom, really – I dabbled with the older, more substantial world of the inner city where the trees were thick-trunked and the grapevines gnarled and the roofs tin and steep with age. Here, old people were staying on and young people moving in to make lifestyle decisions and think long and seriously about themselves. It was the eighties. A quarter acre, fences, another Hills Hoist (the landlord's) in the back yard.

A quintessential Australian suburban life, perhaps. But again, when I dream, when I remember, when I doze into reverie, I don't see the picket fences and the Holden in the driveway. I don't see the checkerboard tiles of the Karrinyup kitchen floor or hear the whine of mowers or the hiss of the boiling chip heater. On rare and dreaded family slide nights, I am shocked to see myself in a glistening yellow raincoat. It was never winter when I was a kid! I never looked so pale! I have to strain to recognize myself in Hush Puppies and a mohair turtleneck, ready for Sunday School with my brother, who is about to bawl. Because in my memory of childhood there is always the smell of bubbling tar, of Pinke Zinke, the briny smell of the sea. It is always summer and I am on Scarborough Beach, blinded by light, with my shirt off and my back a map of dried salt and peeling sunburn. There are waves cracking on the sandbar and the rip flags are up. My mum, brown as a planed piece of jarrah, is reading a novel by John O'Hara with cleavage on the cover and someone is spraying coconut oil on the bodies of girls in wide-side bikinis. Out there is west, true west. The sea is where the sun goes at the end of the day, where it lives while you sleep. I have a fix on things when I know where west is.

I often wonder about these two childhoods of mine, the one contained and clothed, between fences, the other rambling, wind-blown, half-naked between the flags. Is it just nostalgia? Have I idealized these summers and chased their myth all my adult life? Did the suburban boy simply imagine himself a coastal life?

No, I lived both these lives and have the wonky slides to prove it. It's just that I lived the coastal life harder, with more passion. As a kid I recognized that life, embraced it and made it my own. In sight of the sea I felt as though I had all my fingers and toes. I was relaxed and confident. At the beach I wasn't just passive, letting life happen to me; I didn't care about being smart or popular, I didn't long to be better looking. The sea swallowed up all my primary school anxieties. Something suddenly consumed my whole attention. I surged toward shore through the laughing crowd, bodysurfing, careful not to lose the togs. Out beyond the break, I dived and brought up fistfuls of white sand to prove to myself I could do it. The sun on my back was like a blush of recognition, and in the rare moments I was still, I sat and stared towards Rottnest Island, at the wild glitter that bucked and swayed without resting. The remainder of my life was indoor stuff – eating and sleeping and grinding through spelling lists, laps of the oval – but even from school I could see the bomboras breaking way out to sea on a high swell, there at the corner of my eye.

I lived five kilometres inland, a blinding limestone road away from the coast. My house had no view; I was landlocked by picket fences and parked cars and homework, but in the afternoons I could smell the Fremantle Doctor coming in across the treetops, stirring the curtains and the copper-boiled washing. It came as sweet relief, cool and merciful, and at night as it moderated to a gentle breeze it brought the coast upon it in the scents of brine and seagrass. The pounding of the swell against the land's edge was so clear it seemed the sea was only a dune away. I didn't need a map to know where I was. In the atlas I lived in a dot, but with that breeze on my back I had a life and a place.

Chapter Two

A still summer night a world away in a house that smells of cactus and dust and musty kapok. I am six years old and almost asleep in the hollow of the clapped-out mattress. Outside in the Tuesday dark a high tide cracks against the bar at the rivermouth. My skin is pleasantly tight with sunburn and smelling of vinegar. A stubbed toe throbs under the lightness of the sheet. The fridge kicks in and whirrs across the sleeping sounds of my mother, my father, my sister and brother. I am drifting, rising and falling in the early current of sleep when suddenly, above me, there is a snap and a scream that lasts less than a second. Somewhere in the dark a terrible struggle. I lie there transfixed, totally awake now, and something warm dabs onto my forehead.

I hear my mother murmur sleepily and my father scrabbling for his torch. The beam comes on and strays drunkenly around the long room of iron bedsteads and cast-off furniture before finding the shuddering pendulum above me. My mother gasps but does not scream. Snug in its trap, a great dying rat swings from a few metres of cord tied to the rafters, and as it passes in its horrible arc with its hairy whip of a tail a few centimetres above my face, the creature offers up another glob of blood that hits the sheet with the tiniest sound imaginable.

—

For a few summers my family had Christmas holidays in a shack at the mouth of the Greenough River, just south of Geraldton. A strange house in retrospect, to a child it was the most remarkable place to have year after year, and I sometimes think that it was this house that caused me to become a writer. It was certainly the prime cause of my obsession with the coastal life.

Fronting the tea-coloured Greenough and overwhelmed by vast paddocks of hay stubble behind, it was a simple, peculiar shack in a lake of doublegees. The front yard was a dead stretch of buffalo grass upon which stood the most hideous concrete statues of birds and animals, all with marbles for eyes. I gave them a wide berth and often found myself shooting glances at them across my shoulder as I scooted along the big wind-blown veranda.

Out the back was a watertank, high on a

rough jarrah stand, and sheds that contained
the generator and the bucket shower I came
to dread. Further along was the thunderbox
dunny, a place of mystery and fascination, and
a sort of half-open greenhouse crammed with
cactus.

From the front windows you could see out
beyond the eyelid of the veranda to the bright
limestone road and the rivermouth. Out there,
the sand was packed hard and cars could be
driven across between river and sea. The surf
hammered night and day, never calm, never
quiet, blue all the way to Africa.

The house itself consisted mainly of one
huge L-shaped room lined with beds, remnants
of other houses and times and places. They
were a wild assortment and a kid could jump
from one end of the place to the other without
touching the bare concrete floor that was
always adrift with balls of dust and streaks of

beach sand. Under our beds we had boxes of comics — *Archie, Donald Duck, The Phantom, Casper the Friendly Ghost, Richie Rich, Little Lotta* — and there were boys' and girls' annuals from England, books of adventure, scuffed blue-spined novels that smelled of antiquity and fried bacon.

Above us were the rat traps on the bare rafters, and in every corner, under every battered cupboard and gutless armchair, were neat little saucers of Ratsak. In the mornings my father would clear the traps and bury the rats out in the paddock where he emptied the thunderbox, out in the evil field of doublegees where no thong was thick enough to protect you. Dugites and bobtails rustled out there, and in the evenings, bronzed by the sun as it dunked into the sea, whole mobs of kangaroos lined the ridge until they became silhouettes and childish cutouts of themselves in the last of the light.

There was so much mystery in that house. The kitchen was a fairly basic affair – sink, kitchenette, fridge. It smelt of gas and kero, spent matches and rusty cans. The sink emptied into a bucket in the cupboard below and around the bucket were piles of strange little tins that kept all of us gasping as we read the labels. There were sugared ants, Italian anchovies, pâté from England, olives from Spain, and squarish tins of frogs' legs that we hardly dared to handle. The whole cache was shocking and hilarious. Now and then, on a dare, my father would hack a can open and bravely squelch something down, his cheeks red with valour, and he'd murmur with great satisfaction and offer it around. We scattered like gulls.

I never ate anything out of that cupboard,

but I went back to it regularly to work through the contents and wonder at the cities on the labels. These were things from the outside world, somehow potent and terribly exotic. Somewhere there were people who ate this kind of stuff!

There were two other rooms in the shack. One I can only dimly remember as a sort of parlour with a rat-chewed chaise longue and glass cases full of whisky miniatures, ash trays and knick-knacks of the pub trade. The other room, the room that really interested me, was the library. The shack at Greenough was the first house I ever knew to have its own library.

The owners of our beach place were my mother's relatives from Geraldton, Clem and Connie Penniment, former publicans and substantial figures in the port town. As a freckle-faced kid of six I thought they were my uncle and aunt, though I later discovered that they were in fact my great uncle and aunt. Large and imperious, they were also old and rather eccentric. The concrete animals should have told me something. The poor moulting black crow in the cage behind their newsagency might have offered a hint. The rooms of *stuff* above the shop, the fistfuls of brightly coloured tablets they took like so many mixed lollies, the way Uncle Clem looked down at his skiff-like brogues and muttered to me, 'Hm, what d'ye think?' before striding off grandly – and then saying exactly the same thing to me next year. Really, these things should have let me know they were quite unlike the people I knew in my raw little suburb of plainness at home.

What finally sent the message was the library. It was no bigger than a bedroom but it was four walls of books, a world unto itself. There were regiments of books, whole blocks and processions of uniform editions; Somerset Maugham, Dickens, George Eliot, Balzac, Melville, Twain, Mrs Gaskell, Virgil, Homer, Edmund Burke, Galsworthy, J.B. Priestley, Poe. There was a fruity, illustrated edition of *The Decameron* in two volumes, and an early edition of *Mein Kampf*, whose author sounded familiar. Leather spines, dustjackets from the twenties, thirties and forties, pocket editions, bookclub editions, rat-punctured art books, Gilbert and Sullivan librettos, tomes on medicine and the human body. All this finally told me that the tall people who slipped me the odd *Archie* comic on our weekly bread and milk trip were not ordinary people. Ordinary people had a Bible, a set of cheap encyclopaedias, stacks of *As You Were* and *Reader's Digest*; a yarn by Ion Idriess, perhaps, but not all this. This was outrageous, and it was probably just the overflow they couldn't squeeze in at home.

I spent a lot of time in that library. It was there that I discovered Robert Louis Stevenson and then *Robinson Crusoe* and *The Swiss Family Robinson*, the books that snatched me from the world of the *Archie* comic and never quite let me go back. Physical and compelling, these stories were the world of the desert island, the lonely beach, the still lagoon. I read *The Coral Island*, about chaps making do on whatever was to hand, and though I knew for sure that I'd never end up a chap and say 'Grand!' a lot, there was the chance that I could make do quite nicely on crayfish and rabbits and sleep nights in the warm sand. These were the first books that offered me some of the real world I knew, then carried me off completely to somewhere that didn't exist at all. Since then I've lived with a weakness for old-fashioned books from that library on my own shelves today. In many ways I'm still that open-mouthed boy, turning the pages, wanting to know what happens next; who pored, perved, flicked and sniffed his way from wall to wall every afternoon all those years ago.

For the library was an afternoon place. On the west coast in summer the morning is for the beach and the afternoon is a time to find shelter. The western summer is ruled by wind. Here the wind is a despot. It rushes off the land before dawn, ploughing out into the sea, full of wheat dust and pollen, crashing at the curtains and rattling every loose sheet of tin, warm and unrelenting. It heats up with the coming of day, an allergenic blast that scorches flat everything in its path. Wild oats and Paterson's Curse lie down before it. Out of the mysterious interior it barrels to tear the tops from breaking waves and hollow their troughs into glittering cylinders. On a summer's morning the sea smells of the land

and the dunes become airborne. Sand falls far out beyond the smoke of bushfires to become a haze in the water, a puzzlement to fish.

It's morning when people are about, when the sea is bullied flat by the wind and the air is hot and dry. Just before noon the easterly mellows and becomes benign and before long it gives out altogether. The ocean glasses off, cicadas and birds find full voice in the sudden quiet, the coastline briefly becomes Mediterranean. This mild interlude might last five minutes or an hour, but it is never more than a lull, an imitation of gentle weather.

Before long the horizon begins to go wobbly. It stacks up mirages of boats, islands, capes, and the milky sea is streaked with lines of gooseflesh. You can see the Doctor coming in the distance, a ruffling line, an advancing front that curves in from the sou'west. When it arrives, there is a sense of relief, a cool rush of air and a softening of the sea. Then a light chop appears and confuses the surf. People begin to open up their houses. On the beach they shake out their towels and, out at sea, anglers haul anchor because, within a few minutes, beach umbrellas will be uprooted and sand flying as the sea loses its colour and gathers a nasty chop. Great plumes grow from the backs of the dunes and the heathland rattles with the afternoon gale. The sky goes white with sand and the trees on the coastal plain kiss the ground they grow on. The afternoons are the time to be inside on a bed with a book.

Just after dawn on those holiday mornings my father would shake me awake quietly and slip out to make himself a cup of tea. I'd find him in the kitchen scratching his whiskers in the blue glow of the Primus.

Out in the morning breeze he carried a hessian bag of shucked abalone and ham hocks for cray bait. Together we walked down along the mud-smelling river and crossed the crisp white of the bar to head up the bush track behind the dunes. We never said much, just listened to the close sound of our feet in the sand.

Down on the reef at low tide the rock pools and solution holes were brimming pits in the great exposed shelf. Octopus clambered about from hole to hole and startled sweep blurred away as we passed. Out at the edge of the reef where the surf clapped up against its face, the bag was handed to me and my father pulled the jarrah-slat pots up onto the limestone shelf. We snatched out the creaking, twitching crayfish, baited up again, and he heaved the traps back into the deep. Now and then a big swell hit the reef edge and reared up to come charging across the platform at us as a wall of boiling foam. I stood wide-legged and side-on to it as I was taught, holding the waistband of his shorts, feeling the crays kick and butt the bag against my legs. The force of the water was immense and terrible. Sometimes I was blasted completely off my feet, only to feel my father's grip anchoring me to the earth.

Back at the shack, where the rest of the family were stirring, we tipped the crays out onto the concrete floor to let them crawl around in their backward, sleepy manner. The little kids shrieked with delight.

Some mornings I slept in and walked down alone to the reef to meet my father. It felt very grown-up to walk so far on my own. The bush was strangely quiet, the sea a murmur on the reefs. The saltbush was pungent and the light was orange. Rabbits, and once a fox, crossed my path. One morning, when my father had taken the Holden instead of walking, he came hammering up the track flat-out to keep from sinking in the powdery sand and fishtailed around a bend to find me standing in the middle of the track. He swerved, I dived, and we had a few solemn minutes of digging and shunting to get the FC out of the scrub. I trembled all the way to breakfast.

Summer days were long at Greenough. We swam in the river and surfed on the beach when the rips weren't too treacherous. We rowed around the estuary and fished for bream and stood out on the jagged limestone point and baitcast for tailor. Every day my little brother went down to the caravan that served as a shop to try to buy lollies with bits of glass and bottle tops. He had more success some days than others, but at the end of the holidays Mum had to go down and settle his account.

There were horses in a paddock behind the dunes and some mornings my brother and I walked over to watch them. He had a strange fascination with them, a compulsion really. When he was eight or nine he got sick of watching and took to slipping through the fence and mounting them bareback. I watched in a sweat, terrified that he'd be found out and I'd be the one to have my bum kicked, but he only thought of the moment as he rode around with his hands in the scruffy mane like the natural he was.

He was the same in the river. At the edge of the sandbar, where the bank fell away to deep water the colour of tea, he strode out repeatedly, convinced he could swim. My mother dragged him out by the hair and went on with the lesson. That's where we learnt to swim, there in the river, within tantalizing sight of the sea that crashed on the other side of the bar. Swimming is a great mystery, like riding a bike, like reading. Suddenly, after days and weeks of trying and failing, one morning you can do it.

Some mornings when the tide was right out we went onto the reef with screwdrivers to prise off abalone, which we called muttonfish. Dad shucked them and bashed them with a mallet under the tankstand and fried them in butter. We ate tailor, whiting, bream, crayfish and they made up for the frozen bread and milk, the cans of camp pie and baked beans, the dreaded tinned beetroot.

In the afternoons while the seawind brawled in across the rivermouth we lay on our bunks and read. Our noses were peeling, our feet scabby, our hair bleached, our lips chapped. The afternoons were quiet, exhausted, contemplative. Dad read Zane Grey and I remember Mum reading Errol Flynn's *My Wicked, Wicked Ways*. The house was full of the smells of fried fish, vinegar and Coppertone. One year I lay there for three weeks, in the midst of broken Christmas presents and Scrabble tiles, and read

Jules Verne's *Journey to the Centre of the Earth*. It smelt of the library, another world. The print was so small it made me giddy.

When I went to browse in that library someone would have to throw a beach towel over the stuffed eagle in the corner. That bird's eyes were brown and glassy and they followed me round the room. Its upraised wings and fierce beak were threats I recognized in many a library and classroom later on. A kid can't always have a towel handy, but those afternoons I was safe and the world of books opened up to me like a dim shaft into the centre of the earth.

Those summers were both active and contemplative, the weather always fair but never gentle. Morning and afternoon I learned the pattern of my life, of hunting and gathering and picking over flotsam in the outdoor world – fishing, diving, swimming, surfing, lighting fires, rowing boats, feeling the landscape rush in from all sides — and of retiring indoors to wonder and write and read where only the breeze could reach me, in there where my dreams were. I would never be content with only one world or the other. At the time it felt like the ideal life, that coastal summer idyll, and maybe I've lived all my years a hostage to a six-year-old's fantasy.

Chapter Three

Just below me sharks lunge and burrow into a wall of quivering flesh and the sea is pretty with blood. A pall of gulls hangs above the water. A winch grinds into gear. I am fourteen years old and a busload of other fourteen-year-olds clamours around me as the sperm whale is winched up slowly onto the flensing deck at Frenchman Bay. As it comes up, a single bronze whaler, unable to leave off gnashing, is dragged onto the deck snout-deep in blubber. It twists its head, hacking and wolfing, until it loses hold and rolls down the slick wood into the water.

The whale is enormous. Its long, stiff lower jaw lies ajar and its eye seems closed. The glossy black flanks are so vast you can barely see where the sharks have been, but already men are upon it, their flensing knives, like glinting hockey sticks, running deep into the blubber so that in only moments the pearly pink flesh begins to show. Held by the cable, the tail extends rigid, but the flukes have dropped.

Men in beanies and sea boots work away with good humour, conscious of the mob above them. The air is putrid with the steam of boiling blubber. It is the most rancid smell I have ever encountered and here and there along the embankment other kids are retching and heaving.

On the upper deck another whale has its head sawn off. Huge mattresses of blubber are hauled past it toward the vats. A steady drizzle floats in from the Sound, subduing the smell somewhat, while sky and sea take on the colour of a single contusion. I am fourteen and this is a school excursion in Albany, Western Australia.

—

The sea is a field of miracles, a profusion of depths and mysteries. As T.S. Eliot wrote: 'The sea has many voices, Many gods and many voices.' It baffles and infuriates humans because we cannot subdue or comprehensively understand it. We haven't even completely mapped it, let alone explored it.

Australians are surrounded by ocean and ambushed from behind by desert — a war of mystery on two fronts. What worries us about the sea and the desert? Is it scale or simple silence? Historically we see ourselves as outback types, although we know we are suburbanites. Still, we do go to the desert more and more.

We buy four wheel drives and swags and designer gear for camping to make our funny little pilgrimages. From the tent door, or across the motel pool of an evening, we watch the earthly stillness of sunset and we wonder. Yet we head back to the coastal cities that poets such as A.D. Hope used to cane us about. Guiltily we spend the rest of our time living on the water or manoeuvring our way ruthlessly toward it. The desert is a spiritual place, we vaguely understand, and the sea the mere playground of our hedonism.

Robert Drewe has long argued that almost every Australian rite of passage occurs on or near the beach. The beach is where we test and prove our physical prowess, where we discover sex; it is often the site of our adulterous assignations, and where we go to face our grown-up failures. In the end, it is where we retire in the sun to await the unknown.

We are not sea people by way of being great mariners, but more a coastal people, content on the edge of things. We live by the sea not simply because it is more pleasant to a lazy nation, but because of the two mysteries the sea is more forthcoming; its miracles and wonders are occasionally more palpable, however inexplicable they be. There is more bounty, more possibility for us in a vista that moves, rolls, surges, twists, rears up and changes from minute to minute. The innate human feeling from the veranda is that if you look out to sea long enough, something will turn up. We are a race of veranda dwellers and, as Philip Drew writes in his architectural study: 'The veranda is an interval, a space, where life is improvised. The beach, in Australia, is the landscape equivalent of the veranda, a veranda at the edge of the continent.'

From beneath the furrowed brows of our

houses, in the shallows and beyond the surfline, we look out to sea, and things, wonderful things, do turn up.

Nowhere else on the continent is the sense of being trapped between sea and desert so strong as in Western Australia. In many places along this vast and lonely coastline the beach is the only margin between them. From the sea you look directly upon red desert and from the wilderness there is the steely shimmer of the Indian Ocean. There are roos on the beach and shells out on the plain.

Because we have much more landscape and coastline than people, our shores and shallows are still rich in life, diversity and strangeness. We have perhaps more than our fair share of shoreline miracles, of visitations and wonders, and, happily, we haven't destroyed them all yet. In our hunger to control and know everything humans break and spoil. We trash offerings, burn prophets, snub the strange and wonderful. As a schoolboy in Albany I saw this clearly for the first time. A true wonder was dragged up onto a flensing deck and dismantled like a machine in a wrecker's yard, all so it could be rendered into oil and fertilizer. I saw that day what the ocean could produce and was amazed; I realized what humankind was likely to make of such creations and was dumbfounded.

Western Australians are great trashers and thrashers – it's a proud tradition and one we're always threatening to defend by seceding from the rest of the country. A state of small people with big bulldozers. But now and then even we see something that causes us to back off and think before we shoot; little blessings and miracles get through.

Blessings? Miracles? Blame it on a childhood of Sunday Schools if you like. Call them marvels or natural wonders. At the very least they are rare and precious encounters, and some of them are all the more vulnerable, all the more uplifting because they are so public.

Three examples come to mind without a moment's hesitation, all on the same barren stretch of coast, all rare events and inspiration to even the most jaded veranda-sitter.

From the air, the vast shoals and forked peninsulas of Shark Bay are as confusing, as withholding as abstract art. The westernmost tip of Australia defies the eye — whenever you feel a grasp of direction and a sense of perspective coming on, continent becomes island, ocean turns to estuary and you're left confounded. Shark Bay is 28000 square kilometres of enclosed water, the country's biggest estuary.

The land around it looks blotchy and beaten. Desert right to the water, it stains the white beaches vaguely pink. The water is variegated with sandbar whorls, veins of channels, meadows of seagrass like bruises. It's here that Europeans first met the Great South Land – Hartog, Vlamingh, Dampier – and they didn't linger because the landscape seemed to shut its eyes and fold its arms against them; it was inscrutable.

At dawn, though, right at sea level, Shark Bay is just another expanse of water. The beach at Monkey Mia bristles with cotton palms. Silhouetted against the sky is the mast of a moored catamaran. Further up, the skeleton of the jetty. Nothing seems to move. When your eyes adjust you see the distinct line where the water meets the shore – the ever-contested margin of high water.

Then come the silhouettes of people. They're down there already in shorts, pyjamas and wetsuits, with cameras slung, their murmurs welling. Before the first gulp of tea or bowl of Rice Bubbles in tents or chalets or vans, they are down on the beach, waiting.

By the time you muster the will to join them, the sky is fading from purple to mauve, but the coarse sand is still cold underfoot. At water's edge, a man in a wetsuit sits down to haul on an enormous single fin in which there are two sockets for his feet. 'Merde!' he mutters, having a bit of trouble.

Suddenly the hushed crowd erupts. 'They're coming! They're here!'

From tents and across the rolled-out lawns of new 'resort' others come running. Lights are on, doors slam. Someone giggles just this side of hysteria as out on the water a dorsal fin cuts shoreward. The Australian waking nightmare, the dorsal fin. Now another. Then two more.

Pfugh! The sound of a snorkel clearing. *Pfugh! Pfugh!*

A woman shrieks, 'The dolphins are here!'

but the crowd shushes her impatiently and a queer religious hush comes upon them. When three bottlenose dolphins surface and dive in unison, running into the brilliant shallows with the day's first sun glossing their backs, a collective sigh goes up on the beach and the whirr of the videocam begins.

A Japanese man in Tony Llama boots and designer jeans lurches out waist-deep with his great waterpipe of a telephoto lens before him. A dolphin turns its head to cop a look. Hogtied as a hostage, the French man squirms into the water and gets going with his big perspex flipper galumphing on the surface. Two dolphins check him out, make a pass, and head back to the humans. They make a showy sprint by the crowd and peel off separately to return.

In less than a metre of water, three dolphins idle in below thirty outstretched human hands and turn their heads to see. The biggest of them, blotched and scarred, with notches out of its dorsal fin, slips between gasping people, pressing against their thighs. It props on its pectoral fins, arches out of the water, its head turned sideways, and opens its mouth. A half-metre away from you.

You reach out and stroke its side, your arms tangling with those of strangers. The skin is smooth, slick, firm and the body beneath it is heavy. It's bigger than you. This is a wild dolphin; it is not trained, it has never been in captivity and it has no need to come in here with its companions every day of the year. It clicks and presses against you.

This is the only place in the world you can do this naturally, expect to stand in the water before breakfast, in the middle of the morning, just on sunset, and touch a free dolphin, feel its powerful bulk, look it directly in the eye and feel it slide back out of reach unafraid. This is what all these people have caught planes and buses or spent ten hours in a hot car for. Because none of this is normal, and the ritual has gone on since 1964, before 'Flipper', before environmentalism, before the New Age came slinking upon us. Generations of humans and dolphins meeting on the land's veranda.

Just offshore from Exmouth, against the coral barrier of the Ningaloo Reef, you can cruise slowly southward, rolling in the mild swell and encounter odd swirls on the surface of the water that at first you might mistake for the 'footprints' left behind by sounding whales. As you come closer though, you'll see from the flying bridge that the swirl is more than water. The shadow has a body. It turns and a mighty dorsal fin breaks the surface and you see that it's a shark. Eight metres of shark. The tail swings by like a factory gate and already you're fumbling with your goggles and fins, stumbling down to the aft deck and the open transom door, your lungs in the back of your throat.

You crash out into the bottomless blue and see only bubbles and weird-looking jellyfish for a moment. Tiny dustlike bits of plankton ease past, confusing the eye. In fifty-five metres of water you have no sense of scale, nothing to fix onto, so when that small blur appears below you at mid-water you can't immediately tell if it's an anchovy or a nuclear submarine. But as it climbs slowly and evens out you see an opening with small fish hung on the underside of it, and quite suddenly you see it's a shark's mouth, big as the bucket of a steamshovel. The shark alters course and the real shock hits you as you begin to see the size of its body. The colossal flanks are delicately spotted, as mesmeric as an Aboriginal dot painting, and at first sight as intimidating as a ship's hull. Astonishingly silent, unhurried and seemingly in slow motion, but hard work to keep up with for too long. Festooned with remoras, suckers, cleaners, tiny opportunists. Spangled and speckled by the light on the moving surface of the water, it makes you smile around your snorkel.

You take a breath and dive steep into the warm tropic blur to roll onto your back and fin along quietly beneath its pale crowded belly and watch it blot out the sun. Below you, two bronze whalers, tiny with distance, begin to wind their way up toward you as if on submarine up-draughts, and you register them, in your slow glide to the surface, as hardly bigger than the bubbles in your trail. They come within ten metres and hold their circle pattern, interested but not excited, and it's then that you properly understand the size of the creature you've been swimming with. You finally get a true sense of scale with these carnivores in sight. This thing is really, unbelievably big. A plankton eater, harmless, majestic, and willing to swim with you a while as long as you keep your distance and behave yourself. Open-mouthed, it sieves the water and eyes you neutrally. Then slowly, with imperceptible changes to its trim, it tilts away into the deep, tail fin swinging off into the haze below.

You tread water and marvel. Within sight of the shore, you have swum with a whale shark, the ocean's largest non-mammal. Your snorkel blasts clear and pipes the sound of your hoot.

For months at a time near Exmouth, while the whale sharks feed in the warm, rich water of the Ningaloo, this can be a daily event. The reef itself is spectacle enough, but a swim with a whale shark is a world beater, something that awes even those who do it every day.

Between Shark Bay and the Ningaloo Reef is a lonely, gnarled and cliffy coastline where the sea eats the land and the southerly hacks into every crack and hollow. It's tough country down there: salt pans, cattle stations, red dirt. Near a giant stockpile of mined salt that looks incongruously like a snow cap in all that shimmering heat is Cape Cuvier.

In June 1993 a dark mass formed at the base of the high yellow cliffs there and spread like the stain of an oil slick two kilometres long. An unseasonal easterly blew the sea flat, and the water was so clear that onlookers could see the black belt change shape, elongating here, fattening up there, as though it were alive. To seaward, on the perimeter, were other shadows, small mobile blots that moved in on the big mass, causing it to retreat and press up against the cliffbase so close the spectator could now make out what he still couldn't believe. That was no oil slick down there. It was a vast school of fish being herded by tiger sharks, spanish mackerel and Bryde's whales beneath a natural amphitheatre.

What followed for weeks on end was not so much a feeding frenzy as a nonchalant and amiable slaughter before an ever-growing audience. Marine biologists, tourists, fishermen, news crews gathered on the cliffs to watch whales, sharks and pelagics casually taking turns at gliding into the black cloud of anchovies that made space for them the way the weak always will for the powerful. The predators moved open-mouthed through the captive school, cutting a swathe without gnashing or excitement, leaving only a green trail of clear water behind them that closed up again as the terrified fish bunched for security's sake. Those not feeding cruised the perimeter, herding, shaping, intimidating the millions of little fish. Spanish mackerel, tuna and yellowtail kings worked alongside bronze whalers and tiger sharks.

No feeding event on this scale has ever been recorded before in our waters. Every day the theories grew and multiplied, until the wind changed and the school broke up and headed to sea. It was a heavy-handed lesson in the web of life, a display of force and vulnerability, a travelling show that played a month or so and moved on to leave us wondering.

The frenzy at Cape Cuvier, the presence of the whale sharks at Exmouth and (to a lesser extent, thanks to long term studies) the dolphins at Monkey Mia are barely understood phenomena, but ones which must be regarded as privileges to behold. I find them stirring, inspiring, strangely unifying and even religious in their nature. I don't believe there's anything cosmic or divine or morally superior about whales and dolphins or sharks or trees, but I do think that everything that lives is holy and somehow integrated; and on cloudy days I suspect that these extraordinary phenomena, and the hundreds of tiny, modest versions no one hears about, are an ocean, an earth, a Creator, something shaking us by the collar, demanding our attention, our fear, our vigilance, our respect, our help.

After many dives in the Aegean Sea, where most of these things are long lost, the beaches gummed with oil and the sea foul with plastic bags and sewage, where the dynamited deserts beneath the surface are quieter than any inland sea of the Antipodes, I still remain hopeful about the message getting through in the West, even if nature has to become its own propagandist. Because after the last open coast of Australia is tamed, polluted and overfished, what's left except nostalgia and the desert at our backs?

Living in exile on the island of Guernsey, one hundred and thirty years ago, Victor Hugo prophetically wrote of human nature:

Nothing makes him hesitate; no bulk, no obstruction, no consideration of splendid material, no majesty of nature. If the immensities of nature are within his reach he batters them down. This side of God which can be ruined, tempts him; and he undertakes to assault immensity, carrying his hammer in his hand. The future will, perhaps, witness the demolition of the Alps . . . The child breaking his plaything seems to be seeking its soul. Man also seems to be looking for the soul of the earth.

Chapter Four

With the sun on my back and the outboard purring, I head out through the passage in the reef, riding nicely on the fat tide and making a long arc towards the southwest. The sea is smooth and quartzy. Flying fish glide up ahead and abeam, working their fins to get the best plane possible. Out past the little bombora I almost plough across the back of a loggerhead turtle and my companion whistles in relief. The ocean is fairly teeming this morning. It's Thursday and I should be at work, but it's cruelly hot and the sea is too much to resist for another full day. That wonderful truant feeling buzzes through me. The echo sounder bleeps, the hot wind tears at my hair and I keep my bearing.

Several kilometres out I find my spot and my mate drops the anchor. As usual I'm the last in the water, fumbling with excitement. I tumble out into the gentle shock and see the tantalizing swathe of iridescent blue plankton spinning like fireworks, sequins, stars in the sunlight. I squint and train my eyes past this veil till I see the bottom of craggy limestone reef and kelp. My friend, who is two-thirds marine mammal, is down there at fifteen metres already; he trails a silky set of bubbles and his red fins turn lazily.

Out this far there is always a moment of apprehension for every few seconds of pleasure, and that open-ocean shiver goes through me as I take a breath and dive to where the water is cooler, deeper, where the pressure rings the changes through my whole body. I relax, drifting down, feeling the water run over my skin like a tremor of lust. The sea rings and quacks and clicks. My heartbeat is soft and regular. I am gliding, flying, with the country unfolding below.

The speargun creates a slipstream before me. My eyes ache with alertness – the old hunting impulse that hasn't faded since boyhood. Scalyfin and silver trevally turn carefully from me and a breaksea cod hovers above the brow of the reef and the shadows of the overhand are thick with pomfrets, buffalo bream and even a foxfish that lies orange and upside down like a wilful bohemian.

I angle up toward the light, out of breath, the pressure hard in my chest, and at midwater I see my friend hovering patiently as a big, chrome-sided samson fish makes a pass. On the surface I blast out my old air and pant a while, watching the scene below.

My friend taps gently against the steel of his spear shaft and the samson turns, curious. It circles him at a distance and the tapping continues. This fish is all muscle. It eyes the diver and closes the circle to get a better look. The spear flashes — for a moment the same metal colour as the fish — and flies with an eerie, innocent sound. It enters the fish behind the head, high in the shoulder, and my friend heads up for air with line trailing through his hands. This fish is capable of towing him round all day, drowning him if he's not careful. But the shot is too good, the samson shudders and changes colour from silver to yellow, to white to brown, in waves and blotches. Its gills flex and suddenly it coughs up a great gout of squid and small fish which becomes a cloud before its eyes. From every corner of the reef come feeders, scroungers, opportunists who tear into the stuff, unafraid of the twenty-five-kilo monster quivering next to them. The samson heads for the bottom, claiming line, making my friend work hard on the surface. It turns and tries a run but dies before it can get up any speed. As it comes up in its jetstream of blood, I see it has gone bronze, the colour of its death. I feel mixed emotions but I don't think anything noble. I am not at one with the fish. I am in the sea, where I do not belong, where I have never belonged all these years of watching, hunting, collecting, forgetting.

I see my own fish, a baldchin, fluttering between bombies way down, so I take a draught of hot continental air and glide the descent like some predatory bird, making myself small to the eye, coming out of the sun, seeing my chance. I am in the sea but not of it.

—

I learnt to snorkel at Mettams Pool at the age of seven. It was a fine way to see girls' bums underwater and in this regard it never disappointed me. For a while I took far too much notice of cartoons in which a bird lands on the snorkel and lays an egg. I was forever rolling over to survey the sky.

Having a mask, snorkel and fins, I was suddenly unselfconscious in the sea. Face down, I floated without thinking. There were too many other things to notice to bother with 'swimming'. My mother and my snorkel taught me how to swim. As a teenager, having moved with my family to Albany, I learnt to dive in the granite clarity of the Southern Ocean, the home of the great white shark, where the awesome sight of submarine boulders and dropaways sobered me up considerably. Here the ocean was completely consuming; it was a threat with one hand and a gift with the other.

Freediving in the open ocean, for all the other things it is, is mostly a form of forgetting. Surfing, swimming laps, drifting a bait from a jetty or a boat are similarly forgetful things. They are forms of desertion, retreat, hermitage, a stepping-aside from terrestrial problems to be absorbed into the long moment. The sea is immense, trackless, potent, but above all, neutral. I used to console myself with the thought that if the sea drowned me, if a shark took me or a blue-ringed octopus or stonefish or sea wasp had its impersonal way, then at least there was no ill-will involved.

Of all water occupations, freediving is the most forgetful. You turn your back to the land, to the sun, and slide down to where all sound is flattened to chirps and rumbles. The deeper you dive the heavier is the blanket that insulates you. You wilfully forget to breathe; you sidestep the impulse and your thinking thins out to the moment at hand. The poet John Blight had it clearly: 'All reason drowns: drowning in you.' It's a religious feeling. On the seabed, or gliding midwater with everything sharp in focus and my body aching with pleasant, urgent hunger, I understand the Christian mystics for moments at a time. I too feel swallowed, minuscule, ready. The diver, like the monk, however, contemplates on borrowed time. Sooner or later you have the surface to return to.

The sea got me through adolescence, pure and simple. I was loved and supported, maybe even indulged by my parents as a teenager, but I fairly burned with turmoil. I was frustrated, impatient, confused, angry. From thirteen to eighteen it was the tyranny of hormones — what a republic that was!

Surfing and diving became a necessary escape. They burned off dangerous energy and gave me a great release from the entanglements of school, family, the agonies of love and loyalty. I was unsociable but not quite anti-social. The diver's daze, the surfer's daze, they leave you with more than the drunk's daze or the junkie's stupor. Not that what I did was entirely safe. Feeling immortal, I cheated death all the time, diving deeper and deeper, taking risks in caves at the end of my breath limit, pushing that bit further till the fish shimmered and the light wobbled and the final forgetfulness hovered at the edge of vision. Sweet, evil rapture. I wore my nosebleeds like a badge of honour. The teenager is a fascist and a fool as well as a seer.

As I slowly mellowed and became more sociable I spent weeks each year camping along the south coast with friends. In a way, these trips were a kind of living out of my childhood reading: *The Coral Island, Robinson Crusoe, The Swiss Family Robinson*, a harking back to the summer days at Greenough. I lived those weeks as though we had truly been stranded out there at Cheyne Beach, Waychinicup or Cape Riche, and imposed a regime on my poor companions of foraging in the mornings and reading in the afternoons.

We dived for abalone, speared and caught fish, even tried hunting roos and rabbits with spearguns – thankfully without success. We picked over the beaches, walked for hours a day, climbing black granite headlands to come back to camp with firewood, flotsam, food and some kind of communal pride. We had a hell of a time.

In the afternoons, up a tree, in a tent, by the fire, I read *Moby-Dick*, Malcolm Lowry, Faulkner, Henry Handel Richardson, Dickens, Kurt Vonnegut. It seemed like a civilized life, but it always had to end. There was always school, town to go back to.

I met hermits on those trips and observed them respectfully. At Waychinicup I met Frank Cooper who had lived out there on his own since the war. His shack was beside a pristine inlet in the granite that was fed by a freshwater stream. He had a clinker boat and some nets, a woodshed, a fish smoker and a handmade sunflower that birds lit on and turned with their tiny weight in front of his bright-painted tin house. He was ambivalent about company, but I talked with him many times, traded stories and supplies with him. His immaculate compound was almost invisible in the lonely landscape of heathland and granite extrusions. I saw his life as ideal, though I never saw him with a book.

All along the coast I met solitary men in squatters' shacks surrounded by raw bush and sea, and I saw a life for myself out there until I began to sense their fear. I was eighteen before

I saw these quiet, cranky, lonely men as people who had sought refuge and become stranded. There was always a wife, a father, a detective, a boss they were fleeing. They were stuck in time, always in their moment of betrayal or humiliation or outrage. They had stayed too long in their shacks or at some place in their memories, and everyone had forgotten them. Their own forgetting had left them with nothing to go on with. They scrounged furiously for firewood and shot at anything unfamiliar. They were exiles, not hermits the way Frank Cooper was a hermit. Most of them never seemed to even have names anymore. They gave me my first stories and my first novel, then the councils and governments weeded them out, knocked down their shacks, and I wonder what happened to them.

Recently I went back to those bald patches in the bush and found the places changed;

I found myself changed, too, but the white squeaky beaches and the sea were the same.

I lived in a city, finished school and endured university with the coast always close as it mercifully is in Perth. I wrote books, married, had children and travelled. In Europe I tried the landlocked existence. In Paris I experienced my first apartment and my first truly dispiriting body of water, the Seine. The city itself was a revelation, an astounding and beautiful place, but after six months I found myself crazy for the margin. At St. Malo on a freezing, wind-blasted day I stood on the dun beach at low tide with the choppy Channel out there before me and felt enormous relief at the air and sudden space, but I couldn't say I suddenly had my bearings again. Even on the Galway coast, at the cliffs of Moher that reminded me so strongly of Albany, when I at last saw west, recognized the wildness of the weather coast, the familiar loneliness and romance of being at the last edge, I was still hesitant, unsure of myself, troubled. It just gave me a taste for the real thing.

For many years now I have lived in a redneck crayfishing town of six hundred people and seven hundred dogs. I am by turns sociable and reclusive. I have my own library and houseful of kids and I go to the sea every day I can. Those days I can't, I have the smell of rotting seagrass and the blast of the Fremantle Doctor to remind me I'm close. The summer air is white with blowing sand. We live morning and afternoon the way I did as a boy in Greenough. Thank God we don't outlive all of our childhood fancies.

Chapter Five

An endless small boy's night in a sea of dunes silver and pearly with moonlight. Some Good Friday night, before reading and writing, when the moon rides the crests and hides in the troughs as we plough on. My father rides the step of the Land Rover, my mother says nothing. Someone drives, doing all the talk, and the gearbox growls. I drift back to sleep, tucked against my mother who smells of coffee and the rubber seal of the Thermos.

When I wake we are sinking and the vehicle lows and kicks like a drowning steer. The doors crash open and we are out on the dreamy soft-ribbed sand that stretches off like sleep itself. I lie there cool and run my hands through it where the moon spills. Behind me, my father and my uncle bow before the voice of their old mother. Sand flies into the puce sky and there is grunting and swearing as the wheels spin. I could walk off into this silky sand, into the dream of dunes beyond the moon, but someone hoists me up to see the Land Rover toil free and fantail up the final slope until it tips out into the sky and waits there.

—

Dunes have always been strange, hallucinatory places for me, especially at night. From the early memory of thrashing our way toward Wedge Island in the early sixties, I always associate them with dreams and awakenings.

I recall running through dunes south of

Geraldton years later with a cousin. The only sound was our breathing. There was no moon and the undulations were mesmerizing. We tumbled down ridgebacks and blowouts, dizzy and blind with grit, and I began to panic, falling behind. I staggered, fell. I was lost. The sand soaked up my voice and I ran madly on, my cousin out of sight. I could not hear the sea or the wind. I clawed my way up a long, evil hissing slope and saw the light on the lonely beach and my father with a mulloway slung across his back like an aura and I sat at the crest and cried till I couldn't anymore.

From a dune I once saw an uncle running madly from the shallows with an octopus coiling up his leg. It was red like his hair and he was convinced it was after his dick.

I used to dig holes in the moist sides of dunes to stick my head in and listen to the silence. I scared the hell out of myself in dunes, now that I think of it.

Once, while my father caught salmon at Floreat, I ran in the scrubby dunes that went mauve under the lights of West Coast Highway, and stumbled upon a bloke and a girl going at something very strenuous and peculiar in a shadowy hollow. I fell to the sand and lay still, then crawled to the lip of the dune and peered over. I must have started something of an avalanche because the bloke – who had big black sideburns and looked like Oliver Reed – left off his huffing and puffing and reared up, grabbing his jeans, to come roaring up at me. I barely felt the sand beneath the tips of my toes. My father looked startled when I came barrelling into the light of the lamp where salmon jetted bright blood onto the sand.

Driving in dunes I find myself mistrusting every surface, seeing treacherous patches of light drift everywhere, until I'm almost paralysed with indecision. Not a state of mind to be in when you need to be going flat out in order to stay afloat. He who hesitates is lost, as my old football coach used to say, singling me out, I'm sure.

Nowadays I live with dunes more or less at my back door. They are the same dunes I remember as an infant. In the sun they fairly glow. Japanese video clips are often shot there and on occasion I walk out into that contained desert to watch men in black leather trousers miming their songs on some virginal crest with the sun in their eyes. I wonder what they make of all this bare space. I don't guffaw at their miming; I know what it's like to call out in the dunes and be robbed of your voice.

Year after year, the local cops bring bodies out of those dunes. Kids killed in motorbike collisions or falls from impossible slopes.

Middle-aged men who had heart attacks in their beach buggies. Suicides long dead and found by accident.

When I was eight or so I went to the drive-in with my family to see *Lawrence of Arabia*. From behind the rear seat of the station wagon in my jarmies I saw great sculpted dunes like those I knew from Geraldton and Wedge Island and Eucla. There was much cutting and slashing and camel thrashing. There was the disturbing face of Peter O'Toole, whose car I would not have hopped in for all the lollies in Australia had he come lurking round my playground. But the scene I remember fondly is where Lawrence and the merry slashers crest the last dune and arrive at Aqaba. They galumph down onto the beach on their camels and spill into the sea, still in their dressing gowns. The waves break sweetly upon them and they dance gaily about. I cheered for them, mistakenly thinking that the whole film had been an epic struggle, a great journey to find a decent beach and have a swim.

Aqaba!

Who could blame them? Dunes are the promise of a beach after all, and those blokes had endured an unusually long stretch of them. Never mind the dressing gowns, lads, hop in!

Chapter Six

The dinghy skims across the glass of a lagoon one long weekend Saturday in the early autumn. My two cousins sit up in the bow, my dad behind them obscured by cane craypots, while I sit at the transom seat by my uncle who steers the outboard. I am nine years old and consumed by the sight of the reef running so lucidly beneath me. I trail my hand in the water and a little rooster tail lifts behind it.

Out at the Hole in the Wall we idle about, looking for a likely bit of reef, and then the pots and all their rope tumble out into the green hole, leaving a train of bubbles to mark their descent. The floats snug up on the surface and we curve away lighter. The sky is calm as the sea, as unblemished and endless. At the shore, the flat little town has an army of white dunes advancing on it and the island seems to have broken its moorings and come free of the land just this minute because it tilts and bobs at the edge of my vision.

Suddenly the boat swerves and the pitch of the motor rises. I lurch into the gunwale and scramble for a grip and look up to see a great glossy wave bearing down on us. It trundles along silently, lumping the dappled reef in its path, and we begin the long drymouthed climb up its face and launch free into the air at the crest, hanging in a gale of nervous laughter for a second, before crashing down into the trough and the veil of spray behind. But there is another one coming; there will always be another one coming. The aluminium hull vibrates. My uncle swears and steers full throttle. This wave is feathering, getting ready to break, and we tear up its dizzy front and blast sickeningly out the other side into the path of something much bigger. There is shouting and contradictory pointing of fingers. The prop cavitates, trying to get a grip on the sea. The wave blots out the sky, its lip falling already, like a detonated factory wall, and we turn hope-lessly to run before it, to beat it to deeper, safer water. I feel the foam at my back and see the long horrendous downhill run before us as the wave gathers us up and propels us on.

'Hangin' five!' yells my jaunty cousin in the bow.

Then it's just bubbles; silence and a corona of bubbles that billows blue about my head. I gaze about dreamily until I understand. I am underneath the upturned boat with thirty kilo-gram line floating around my legs and I am drowning. My head butts against the seats. Out in front of me my fingernails are pearly and beautiful. From under the gunwale comes an arm. I watch it with grave disinterest and the fat glossy bubbles part before my rushing face.

—

I love the sea but it does not love me. The sea is like the desert in that it is quite rightly feared. The sea and the desert are both hungry, they have things to be getting on with so you do not go into them lightly. Never turn your back on the sea, my father told me when we fished the rocks at Parry Beach or Greenough or Gull Rock. I never go to sea, fishing wide for jewfish or pelagics, without that frisson of concern that makes my fingertips electric for a few moments every day. I often fish alone so I'm conscious of how vulnerable I am, what a speck I am out there. I am not superstitious but some days I just don't press my luck.

Out on my own one autumn, with a busted finger and no gaff, I worried a sixteen kilo jew-fish to the surface on eight kilo tackle. After half an hour it lay exhausted on its side ten metres out from the boat. I tickled it toward me with forensic care, saw the frayed and savaged trace and reached for its gills. I hesitated a moment and looked seaward, out of reflex, then heaved it over the side, almost tipping myself out, and headed for home without delay. It was almost too good to claim without retribution; I went back with an open throttle.

The ocean is the supreme metaphor for change. I expect the unexpected but am never fully prepared. Suddenly, from a mirror-smooth sea, a pod of randy humpbacks starts leaping and crashing around you. Out in the channel you feel the cold grip of cramp as you swim for shore. Climbing up a slick granite slope with your fins in your hand and the dive weights slung over your shoulder you hear the terrible surge of the freak swell behind you. Beyond the flags and the laughing families, with the city spiking behind them, you labour in the rip, feeling your calm, your cool, ebb away.

Australians do not go to 'the seaside' the way the English do. We go to the beach with a mixture of gusto and apprehension, for our sea is something to be reckoned with. We are reared on stories of shark attacks, broken necks from dumpings in the surf, and the spectre of melanoma. I suspect we go because of these warnings, at times, and not simply despite them. The sea is one rare wild card left in the homogenous suburban life. Deep down we still see ourselves as goers. Being last out of the water after the shark siren, taking the biggest wave of the set, coming home with the meanest sunburn, right to the bikini line — these are still badges of honour.

There are times when the size of the ocean and its overwhelming ambivalence become dispiriting. You look up from the sink of dishes and your mild, happy thoughts and glance at the sea, sometimes, to have your mind go suddenly, unpleasantly blank. Whatever you were thinking just doesn't stack up against the sight of that restless expanse out there. It's like the soundless television, the windbent tree, the campfire, in that it draws you away, divides your attention. At certain moments it's like a memory you are trying to avoid. You stand there, hands dripping suds, looking for whatever it was your eye sought at first glance, but there's nothing there. Just the chafing movement and the big blue stare coming right back at you.

When I think of sleep or coma or fever or death, the ocean comes to mind. Is what we look out at from our retirement deckchairs and our corporate rooms-with-a-view the prospect of unconsciousness, rest, annihilation? Are we longing for release or anxious about being taken? Or are we stuck somewhere between? Would we be more comfortable at the sight of roads, fences, buildings, billboards, cultivated paddocks? A glance up at signs of our terrible success does not divide us so from our train of thought. For every moment the sea is peace and relief, there is another when it shivers and stirs to become chaos. It's just as ready to claim as it is to offer.

Twenty years after my experience out on the reef under the capsized boat, I came to live in that same flat little town. A glutton for punishment, I suppose.

One summer my youngest son, who didn't

swim yet, played in the coral lagoon behind the island while the rest of us lay on the hot sand watching the sea lions. He saw a nudibranch float by, tiny, crimson and purple, just wallowing as they do, in the current. Nearby, hanging off its anchor over the edge of the reef, was the boat. The toddler's sunbleached head bobbed and turned, following the nudibranch toward the big hole in the reef. Before the edge of the deep, he stopped, as taught, but behind him a new current yawed the boat on its anchor. I looked up to see the leg of the outboard shunting him silently and irrepressibly toward the edge. By the time I got to him he was over the dropoff, pedalling in freefall, his blonde hair just in reach. In the sunniest family moment, a silent change; death waiting.

The same summer a deckhand found a friend of ours floating face down in the bay.

A fortnight before this he had told me he 'swam like a stone'.

To complete my ragged little life circle . . . One summer in the nineties I was heading out with my neighbour, Charlie Youngs, with a boatful of pots in a choppy sea when a lumpy, windblown wave reared up before us. We ground into it and out the other side to confront the inevitable follower, which broke just as we reached it and took me and the windscreen with it. I saw that same haze of bubbles, heard that same sudden quiet and then I popped up in time for the third wave to come down on my head and send me bouncing across the reef.

When I finally surfaced and got my bearings, I saw Charlie out beyond the surf, madly bombing pots off left and right to save the boat. He was shin-deep in water and, miraculously, the outboard still ran. The boat was half submerged and the sea was running against the bare barrier of the reef just behind it. For a while I swam in my tee-shirt and shorts till the shirt began to drag on me, so I shrugged out of it, dodging breakers as I did, and balled it up in my fist to swim on. After a couple of minutes of one-handed swimming I thought about the value of the shirt, which cost me one pound on London's Oxford Street some time ago, and hadn't been much of a bargain at that. The pain of my cuts and bruises came upon me. My coccyx burned and throbbed where I had clipped the cowling of the outboard – narrowly spared the horror of the prop. I threw that damn shirt as far as I could and struck out through the surf to the wallowing boat.

That night I dreamed and sweated. I was under a boat in blue bubbles there was no God-like hand to haul me free.

Chapter Seven

On a stifling Sunday morning in the church on the hill I fidget in my pew, eleven years old in my Sunday best, and listen again to the story of Moses. Moses, whose first cradle was a tiny boat in the bulrushes, who led the Hebrews out of bondage and defied the armies of the Pharaoh. Moses, for whom God peeled back the Sea of Reeds to let the slaves cross in safety.

The voice drones on into the years in the Wilderness, but I stay there in the Sea of Reeds; I can't get past that part. The sea folds back to make a path. I imagine those great, quivering walls of water either side of me, the overwhelming smell of brine and iodine. I know, at age eleven, that I would be the Hebrew who wouldn't make it across to the other side. The others would bolt and slide and splash across to dry land, but I, forever the beachcomber, would stoop down and go foraging. Think of the wonderful things hidden from view since the beginning of time: the strange, pressure-flattened creatures that never see daylight, shells, shocked worms and slugs, wreckage from ships and lost cities. The parapets of water are shaking above me, poised and heavier than whole countries, and there I am turning things over, rubbing the silt off them and holding them to the light while the Egyptian horsemen come thundering. And behind me, good old Dad stuffing his pockets with fish, unable to help himself and muttering about the Depression.

A blowfly butts against the wall. The sermon goes on without me, and through the windows comes the hot-bread breeze that heads for the sea just out of view.

—

Perhaps I go beachcombing simply to keep the sea in view. Where I live, if I don't see the ocean every day, even if it's just the eight a.m. ritual of rolling by the jetty for a minute where everyone in this town seems to gather before work to see the state of things, then I become restless and anxious. I have the same feeling if I don't have a book to read, or when I haven't worked for several days in a row. In the city, I'm the kind of driver who goes the long way in order to cop a look at the beach, just a peek between Norfolk pines, past the spine of a built-up hill. Each sighting fuels me for the next. I just never get tired of looking at the sea. I don't quite know what it means to be constantly looking outward. I am not restless to travel or longing for the Europe of my ancestors. I feel part of the land I live on, but I still stare out at the blinding field. And so do others, from every jetty, headland and carpark along the coast.

Beachcombing combines this obsession with the habit of scavenging. A long bare beach, like the sea itself, is capable of many surprises. The unexpected is what I'm after when I go trudging along the firm white sand with not a building or human in sight. True, I'm after solitude as well, and enough sameness to give me the peace to think or maybe sing without feeling self-conscious. But it's the possibility of finding something strange that keeps me walking.

I collect floats, rope, seaboots, the usual jetsam from fishermen who still treat the sea as their marine dispose-all. I pick up the murderous six-pack loops, the plastic straps, the crap that washes up season after season. This year I came upon a TV washed up inside Fence Reef. It looked like an exhibit in one of those Emperor's-new-clothes art shows. Even the dog looked doubtful about it.

Driftwood in bizarre shapes finds it way atop high buttresses of weed thrown up after storms, parts of foreign-looking trees, packing cases with Cyrillic script or Japanese characters. Whole fields of blue-bottles lie stranded, bursting underfoot like little landmines. Sponges, great limbs of coral, sea cucumbers. The wind and the huge Leeuwin current drive many creatures out of their way: one year a vast hatch of baby loggerhead turtles from the Kimberley, another year a leopard seal, exhausted and dangerously cranky after his extraordinary swim from Antarctica.

From a distance every found object is merely a black mark on the sand, and half the pleasure of beachcombing lies in wondering, anticipating the find. What you expect to be a message in a bottle is the half-buried carcass of a sea lion. What you thought was a bleached branch is a whalebone. What you thought was a stingray is that bloody tee-shirt you threw away trying to save yourself last week.

Everything you find looks ancient and mysterious. Things brought home from the sea and its margins become emblems, talismans to the beachcomber. Beach shacks are full of this stuff; it's a kind of kitsch beyond taste. The crossed whalebones over the door, the abalone shells and bleached corals, like dead fingers and brains, on dressers and bookshelves. Smooth stones, pieces of glass, dried seahorses, the skeletons of boxfish and jaws of small sharks. You can only sneer at it if you've never felt that sense of bounty, of excitement, stooping to pick up something that breaks the bareness of the beach, the loneliness of the morning, like a small gift.

My wife sees me coming and rolls her eyes. My trouble is, I keep everything. A critic once called me a 'literalist', which delighted me. For, despite his faulty spelling, he got me right; I am a 'littoralist', someone who picks over things at the edges.

Yet however comforting and peaceful beach-combing is, it ends up, like the sea, as disturbing as it is reassuring. In dark moments I believe that walking on a beach at low tide is to be looking for death, or at least anticipating it. You will only find the dead, the spilled and the cast-off. Things torn free of their life or their place. It can be a melancholy business coming upon the dead pilot whale, the plaintive single oar, the shell that signifies both death and homelessness. The beachcomber goes looking for trouble, for everything he finds is a sign of trouble.

The writer is the same; without trouble he has nothing to work with, so he picks over the tide line, over the bits and pieces of people's lives with grim fascination.

The poet John Blight, in *A Beachcomber's Diary*, writes:

I am ever seeking the quieter beaches.
Do not believe, in Australia, there are miles
where at dawn you will not see the 'prints –
not on the East Coast, leastwise. Here reaches
of sand are scarred from daybreak, the tiles
of footprints are laid down, the dents
made by feet in the sand are there; so stale to me,
such beaches seem no longer virgin to we few – we
people who do not want to meet each other, ever.

In the west, with so much coastline and so few people, it is a simple matter to find these beaches if you leave the city. There are still places to be alone and have the mariner's sensation of being merely a speck. West coasts tend to be wild coasts, final coasts to be settled, lonelier places for being last. In Australia the east coast is the pretty side, the Establishment side, the civilized side. It tends to be well watered and blessed with safe anchorages. It is hilly and offers views. It is the social coast, the sensible coast, at times the glamour coast. As in Ireland and America, our west is seen as something of a new frontier, remote and open.

Our west coast is mostly a flat and barren affair, blasted by trade winds, vegetated with scrub and heath, drifting with dunes. It doesn't lend itself to the picturesque and its squat little towns with their fish-deco architecture barely rise above sea level. These towns, many hundreds of kilometres apart, are the domains of the temporary dwelling: the asbestos shack, the transportable, the gimcrack kit home. The tallest things in these places are the Norfolk Island pines, from whose pencil tips you take your mark at sea or from the desert. The landscape and the merciless weather, the irregular water, never gave white people a sense of the long term; settlers never held out much hope for the future, so they built shacks and sheds until the crays, the whales, the pearl shell, the scallops ran out. The only beautiful towns on the west coast are ghost towns, the pearling ruins of Cossack in the far north and the flood-ravaged hamlet at Greenough. With their handsome stone buildings and charming churches, these seem to have been an early warning against optimism and the chimera of permanence.

West coasters live in the teeth of the wind. Distance, waterlessness, relentless weather have made them taciturn. If you do meet them on that virginal beach John Blight speaks of, they won't detain you long. Fishing makes them secretive; they fear greenies, people from the government, visitors with a rod and reel. Their humour is black. 'You've never been crook till you've thrown up a turd', they'll tell you with a grin as you heave over the side of their boat.

They wear clothes all year that others only wear on holiday. Their faces are crusty with cancers and they give little away with their smiling faraway stares. They are not romantic people and this is not a romantic coast. They feel forgotten, neglected, put upon, and yet proud to be far away, on the edge. But in truth, they are less different than they imagine.

With my mind fixed on the beach since childhood, I am one of them; a mutant version perhaps, but touched enough by what E.J. Banfield called 'those inherent instincts of savagedom – joy and patience in the chase, the longing for excitement and surprise, the crude selfishness, the delight in getting something for nothing.'

The sea brought new people here, driven by the Roaring Forties onto the cays and reefs that lie just below the surface. Australia was 'discovered' by Dutchmen who failed to hang a left, who waited a day too long to come about and ply north for Batavia. They met the land in terrible midnight rendings, in screaming and the grabbing at flotsam, and the land that saved them appalled them. The coins and clay pipes and pots of those wrecks lie stashed in many a fibro house along this coast. Plundered booty from Dutch wrecks is the outlawed form of beachcombing. The blasting of reefs is behind us, but the relics are still salted away. They are sobering souvenirs. When they come out of desk drawers and from behind wardrobes, unwound from their swathes of cotton wool, they are strangely hard to handle, almost unpleasant to touch.

My week is shaped by weather and tide. In

shops and on verandas the state of the sea will give me conversations where they mightn't otherwise exist. I live the split-shift life I learned at the mouth of the Greenough River: outside in the mornings, inside when the breeze comes in. I work indoors and am mostly fiddling away at interior things, but several times each day I catch myself looking outward, squinting for something on the horizon. From my fibro house I see the dunes that I seem never to have been without. I fish and dive and the sea is still rich as my memory of it. I am small and I know it and am grateful to have it spelled out to me week after week by the shifting sea and the endless land at my back. Gifts and signs wash ashore here on the hard white beach, and I stoop with my kids, some days, and pick them up and hold them to the light.

ACKNOWLEDGEMENTS

The author acknowledges his debt to the following works: *Australian Seashores* by W. J. Dakin, Angus & Robertson, 1980, used with permission; *The Confessions of a Beachcomber* by E. J. Banfield, Lloyd O'Neil, 1908, 1974; 'Footprints', from *A Beachcomber's Diary* by John Blight, Angus & Robertson, 1952, 1987, reproduced with permission; *Veranda* by Philip Drew, Collins/Angus & Robertson, 1993; 'The Dry Salvages' by T. S. Eliot from *The Four Quartets*, Faber and Faber Ltd, 1944, used with permission; *The Toilers of the Sea* by Victor Hugo, Heritage Press, 1961; *Veranda: Embracing Place* by Philip Drew, Angus & Robertson, 1992, used with permission.